BANBURY
PAST & PRESENT

High Street, demonstrating the traffic congestion that often made the street unpleasant and dangerous, 1973. A distinctive Midland Red bus brings shoppers in from the Easington suburb which was developed after the First World War. At nos 2 and 3 Littlewoods and Macfisheries had replaced Chapman's the drapers and the Talbot Hotel, representing the steady trend by which national stores gradually ousted local businesses.

BRITAIN IN OLD PHOTOGRAPHS

BANBURY
PAST & PRESENT

MALCOLM GRAHAM &
LAURENCE WATERS

SUTTON PUBLISHING LIMITED

OXFORDSHIRE BOOKS

Sutton Publishing Limited
Phoenix Mill · Thrupp · Stroud
Gloucestershire · GL5 2BU

First published 1999

Title page: The east end of the High Street,
late 1930s (*detail*).

British Library Cataloguing in Publication Data
A catalogue record for this book is available from the
British Library.

ISBN 0-7509-2101-3

Typeset in 10.5/13.5 Photina.
Typesetting and origination by
Sutton Publishing Limited.
Printed in Great Britain by
Ebenezer Baylis, Worcester.

CONTENTS

The Great Western railway station, *c*. 1905. Watched by anxious passengers, railway employees hurriedly load baskets and hampers into the goods van before the train is due to leave.

INTRODUCTION

To Marjory Lester, arriving in Banbury in 1920 at the age of six, the place seemed like something out of a fairy story with its old shops and houses: 'The town was quiet and peaceful, except on market days, when it was all bustle and noise, with farmers and their wives and carriers' carts driving into town and cattle and sheep in the streets.' Her childhood memories were of a traditional Banbury, the market centre for an area that has been described as one of the most fertile farming regions in Europe. In 1854 almost 300 carriers attended the town's weekly markets and they came from every community of significance within a radius of about 12 miles, the area traditionally known as Banburyshire. Cattle were driven in to be sold in Cow Fair, the modern Bridge Street, sheep were sold in Horse Fair and pigs outside the Angel in the Market Place. Corn dealing inspired the building of two rival Corn Exchanges in 1857 and, in 1900, Banbury still had horse fairs in January and September, and a hiring-cum-pleasure fair in October. This world is nostalgically portrayed in old photographs but the reality was less picturesque. On market days, the streets were filthy with dung, people caught ringworm from the cattle and drovers often used heavy sticks to drive their animals into town. Cattle would sometimes escape and charge through the streets and George Herbert recalled an incident in High Street when a bullock burst into a sweet shop, walked round the counter and jumped back through the window, taking the frame with him and scattering sweets all over the place.

Banbury's traditional trades and industries grew almost entirely out of the products of agriculture and stock rearing. William Camden described Banbury's major products as cheese, cakes and ale in 1610 and the last two remained important until recent times. Woolstaplers, millers, corn and seed merchants, sacking manufacturers and oil cake merchants have all flourished in the town. The cloth trade was first recorded in Banbury in the thirteenth century, and during the eighteenth century the town became well known for weaving cloths for horses' harnesses and trappings and for the manufacture of a velvety cloth called plush or shag. The arrival of the Oxford Canal in 1778 probably boosted these industries for a time and the canal fostered the growth of lime-kilns, coal, timber and stone yards; a boat-building yard, eventually Tooley's Boatyard, opened at the end of Factory Street in 1790. The making of agricultural implements, initially for the local market, developed out of the town's ironmongery and millwrighting trades but the industry took on a new dimension in the mid-nineteenth century. James Gardner, an ironmonger in High Street, laid the foundation for the industry especially with the invention of his turnip cutter in 1834 and he established a small foundry in what is now George Street in 1839. He died in 1846 but the German-born entrepreneur, Bernhard Samuelson, acquired the business three years later and transformed it into the Britannia Works, utilising foreign technology and the techniques of mass production to create a major industrial enterprise. The workforce rose from 27 in 1849 to 500 by 1870 and the firm's products were exported, for example, to Russia and Italy. The railways, reaching Banbury in 1850, contributed to the success of the Britannia Works and smaller firms by providing swift access to more distant markets.

The population of Banbury, including Neithrop, rose from 3,810 in 1801 to 11,700 in 1871 but the town stagnated thereafter. Banburyshire as a whole suffered from the Agricultural Depression and the textile industry was in terminal decline in the later Victorian period. Hunt, Edmunds Brewery continued to expand but it was largely at the expense of other local breweries such as Austin's in North Bar. Samuelson's failed to diversify effectively, lost its ability to innovate and faced increasing competition for existing products such as mowing machines. Many local people left the area or emigrated in search of employment, and in 1890 J.L. Langley counted nineteen empty houses in one block on The Causeway. At the time of the 1891 census nearly 10 per cent of Banbury's houses were uninhabited.

The transformation of Banbury began in the 1920s. After the First World War Banbury Corporation bought land on the corner of Warwick Road and Southam Road for a cattle market but, because it was distant from the railway, a syndicate of stock traders, Midland Marts Ltd, preferred a site in Grimsbury. Sales of cattle by auction were transferred to the new yard in 1925 and private sales followed in 1931, leaving only the weekly provision market and the October pleasure fair in the streets. In the late 1920s the Northern Aluminium Co. Ltd chose Banbury as the site for a rolling mill and members of the Corporation bridged the gap between the company's offer and the selling price of the site in Southam Road. The factory opened in November 1931 with just 200 employees, but the works were extended in 1938 and the workforce reached 2,300 during the Second World War. Worried about over-reliance on one industry, Banbury Corporation established a new industrial estate on Southam Road in the 1950s and this attracted a wide range of industries including General Foods Ltd, formerly Alfred Bird & Sons, and Automotive Products Co. Ltd. The town welcomed 'overspill' families from London and Birmingham and proposals to expand the population of Banbury to 70,000 were narrowly defeated in 1966. Growth has continued at a slower pace and over 41,000 people now live in a very much larger town. The opening of the M40 in 1991 has also encouraged further industrial development by placing Banbury at the heart of the motorway network. By 1966 Margaret Stacey remarked that Banbury seemed more like an industrial town than a market centre; in 1998 the sudden closure of Banbury Cattle Market, formerly described as the largest in Europe, confirmed the altered status of the town.

Twentieth-century developments have profoundly affected the appearance and character of the town. The 'fairy story' streets of old shops and houses have been changed by a retailing revolution which has seen small, locally owned businesses largely replaced by supermarkets and branches of national firms. Many older buildings survive above modern shopfronts in Banbury's main streets and the facades of historic properties on the north side of the Market Place were retained during the development of the Castle Shopping Centre in the mid-1970s. Bridge Street, by contrast, has been changed almost beyond recognition since the 1960s and most recently in 1998 by demolition for the new Castle Quay Shopping Centre. Away from the principal streets change has been still more dramatic, obliterating much of old Banbury in the interests of slum clearance, traffic management and commercial development. The Castle Street area has been almost completely redeveloped and the former Town Hall in Lower Cherwell Street is one of the few old buildings left in the once-populous area south of Bridge Street. For older Banburians these changes have been hard to bear, but the town centre has benefited from pedestrianisation since 1991 and more recent developments have tried to respect the character of the place. Outside the town centre the heart of Neithrop has been radically reshaped and, as the population of Banbury has expanded, roads and houses have spread out into the countryside on every side. Before the 1930s Banbury was a place where you knew everyone and you knew where you were; in today's town, that is no longer the case.

Photography in Banbury began in the mid-1840s when Heeley, the Daguerrotype licensee for Cambridgeshire, settled in the town. He introduced the shoemaker, George Herbert, to the art of photography but he secured little business in Banbury, being afraid to advertise in case he attracted the attention of his creditors back in Cambridge. Heeley soon left but at least sixteen other professional photographers are known to have worked in the town between 1850 and 1920. They included G. Anthony Beales who operated at 5 South Bar between 1888 and 1911, and Blinkhorn's which took over Beales' studio by 1915 and still flourishes at the same address. Between them, these photographers will have recorded many local people and places but only a small fraction of their work survives. Another Banbury man, B.R. Morland, a stationer at 31 Market Place, took interesting photographs of the town in the 1900s and he was perhaps one of the growing band of amateurs who were being attracted into photography as it became a cheaper and more accessible hobby. The Oxford photographer, Henry Taunt (1842—1922), first recorded Banbury in the late 1870s and Frank Packer, from Chipping Norton, took more than eighty pictures of the town between the wars. Francis Frith and G.W. Wilson included Banbury in their national photographic surveys and, more recently, photographers working for the *Banbury Guardian* and the *Oxford Mail* have recorded the local scene for those newspapers.

These collections, illustrating the development of Banbury from the 1860s, have helped to provide the old photographs for this book, but the pace of change is so fast that many of the 'old' pictures were only taken a few years ago. Indeed, it has proved necessary to re-shoot some of the new pictures several times during the preparation of the book because parts of the town are changing day by day. The new photographs were taken by Laurence Waters between November 1998 and January 1999 and they form a valuable record of Banbury on the eve of the new Millennium.

ACKNOWLEDGEMENTS

Unless otherwise stated, the old photographs in this book are from the Oxfordshire County Council Photographic Archive, Central Library, Westgate, Oxford (tel. 01865 815432) and Banbury Museum. The images in both collections are currently being digitised and access to them will be a feature of the new Banbury Museum. We are indebted to Keith Price, Picture Editor at Newsquest (Oxfordshire) Ltd, and Paul Langer, Editor of the *Banbury Guardian*, for access to their photograph libraries and for permission to reproduce the images listed below. We would also like to thank Andy Cox, photographer at the *Banbury Guardian*, for his help and Graham Wilton and Martin Blinkhorn for permission to use photographs. Martin Allitt of the Centre for Banburyshire Studies and Chris Kelly at Banbury Museum have kindly checked the text for accuracy but any errors that remain are entirely the responsibility of the authors.

Photograph credits are as follows: *Banbury Guardian*: pp. 20, 34 top, 55 top, 65 top, 70 top, 71 top, 120 top, 130 top, 133 top, 134 top, 137 top, 138 top, 143 top; Martin Blinkhorn: p. 88 top; Newsquest (Oxfordshire) Ltd: pp. 2, 16 top, 17 top, 36 top, 39 top, 44 top, 45 top, 50 top, 51 top, 52 top, 53 top, 57 top, 61 top, 66 top, 67 top, 69 top, 72 top, 73 top, 74 top, 77 top, 81 top, 92 top, 96 top, 100 top, 104, 108 top, 114 top, 115 top, 116, 118 top, 122 top, 123 top, 124 top, 144 top; and Banbury Fare/Four Shires Magazine: p. 103 top.

CHAPTER ONE

BANBURY CROSS TO THE MARKET PLACE

Banbury Cross and some determined onlookers in the early 1900s. The cross was designed by John Gibbs of Oxford and was built in 1859–60 to commemorate the marriage of Queen Victoria's eldest daughter, the Princess Royal, and Prince Frederick William of Prussia. It was thought to be, but is not, on the site of one of Banbury's medieval crosses destroyed by Puritans in the early seventeenth century. Gaslights were placed around the Cross in 1888. To the right, the offices of Banbury Board of Guardians were built in 1900–1.

The removal of the Cross as a traffic hazard was discussed in 1927 but the 'roundabout system' was introduced in 1930 and is still in use. Statues of Queen Victoria, Edward VII and George V were added to the Cross in 1914 and the railings were removed in 1927, making it easier for revellers to climb the structure. The Board of Guardians' offices became Banbury Museum in 1981.

Farmers and dealers gather round the sheep pens in Horse Fair in the late 1870s. Sheep sales were held in High Street until 1656 and the top end of High Street down to the White Lion was known as Sheep Street until the nineteenth century. Traders moved reluctantly to Horse Fair but the area outside the George and Dragon became the established place for weekly sheep sales. The premises of the printer J.A. Taplin are visible away to the right at no. 29 next to the Woolpack pub.

Sheep sales and their attendant smells were cleared out of Horse Fair in 1931 and a public convenience in local stone now stands outside the former George and Dragon. Car parking takes up some of the space but pedestrians have a tastefully paved area complete with seats from which they can watch the world go by.

Banbury Cross and Horse Fair, August 1933. A car keeps left around the Cross and a woman ambles casually over to the structure. The statue of Queen Victoria, installed in 1914, looks down upon the scene and road signs point the way for eagle-eyed motorists. The single-storey County Garages are visible on the left.

Banbury Cross, restored in 1979, is now the centrepiece of a more formal roundabout but it is a quieter spot since the opening of the M40 in January 1991. Pedestrians are now encouraged to cross Horse Fair by a pelican crossing near the modern street lamp. The County Garages building was redeveloped in tasteful neo-Georgian style in 1989. Further along Horse Fair the Whateley Hall Hotel incorporates parts of the former Three Tuns inn; the block also houses the ABC cinema which opened as the Regal in October 1940.

Congestion at Banbury Cross, 1970. A pedestrian steps boldly between waiting cars and a queue of vehicles extends along Horse Fair and round into High Street. A bypass around Banbury was 'in the early planning stages' in 1954 and Oxfordshire County Council identified the need for a motorway from Oxford to Birmingham via Banbury in 1965. While these schemes remained only on paper, traffic conditions in Banbury got steadily worse.

Since the opening of the M40 in January 1991 Banbury Cross has become a pleasanter spot and a flowerbed beside it has improved the setting of the structure from the north and east. A pelican crossing in Horse Fair, replacing the old zebra crossing, seeks to ensure that motorists do not take advantage of the quieter town centre.

The George and Dragon on the corner of Horse Fair and High Street, 1963. First recorded in about 1782, the George and Dragon was a large coaching inn and the carriage entrance led through to a yard and extensive stabling. In the early nineteenth century several London coaches changed horses here and there was a pool outside in which muddy horses could be washed. Beyond the pool, which was later filled in, pens were set up every Thursday for the sheep market held in Horse Fair until 1931.

The George and Dragon closed in about 1970 and the building was later modernised and adapted as a branch of Barclays Bank. The carriage entrance has vanished and a new entrance door with a handsome pediment has replaced the corner doorway. Many of the windows are new and the façade is now smoothly rendered.

Houses at the north-west corner of Horse Fair, 1904. The street was first recorded as Horse Market in 1525 and as Horse Fair in 1626. Horses were sold here for centuries, and in 1900, for example, the January horse fair lasted four days. The occupants of these fine stone houses would have had a grandstand view of such occasions when the best horses were sold on the first two days, second class horses on day three and the cheapest horses and donkeys on the last day, the so-called Gipsy Day.

Church House, newly converted into a restaurant and bar. Church House was built on the site of the old houses in 1904–5 to provide St Mary's Church with a fine public hall. It was designed by W.E. Mills and is built of Hornton stone in an attractive late Gothic style. For seventy years the building was a social centre for Banbury, providing a venue for dances, whist drives, concerts, wedding receptions, lectures, amateur dramatics and school Christmas parties.

A quiet afternoon in North Bar, *c.* 1930. Advertisement hoardings cover the façade of Percy Gilkes' newsagent's shop at 32 Parson's Street where a dog stands guard by a parked bicycle. In the early 1920s Stranks' restaurant was a popular stopping point for men driving new cars from the Midlands to London showrooms; by this time it had blossomed into a hotel but still offered breakfasts, lunches and teas and catered for coach parties. Beyond Stranks', a gateway provided rear access to the Buck and Bell at 39 Parson's Street.

Dillons now occupies 32 Parson's Street where paint has obliterated the Victorian brickwork; blocked windows are still a reminder of the old adverts. A new Buck and Bell was built on the site of Stranks' in 1935 after the old pub in Parson's Street was converted into two shops.

William Arthur Truss's fish shop at 41–42 Parson's Street, *c.* 1930. Truss started his business at no. 42 in the early 1920s and supplied the Horton Infirmary with fish on Fridays. His fish and chip shop, prominently advertised by a bracketed lamp, had a basement kitchen; fish and potatoes were lowered through a trapdoor and hauled up again later ready to eat.

Truss's business continued at nos 40–41 until the mid-1980s. Oriental food is now on sale at nos 40–41, reflecting the more cosmopolitan nature of modern Banbury; and computers are on offer at no. 42.

Parson's Street, looking east past the Reindeer Inn, 1920s. The bust of Shakespeare was formerly a pub sign for the Shakespeare Tavern which flourished between about 1869 and 1903; the building later became a registry for domestic servants. On the right, beyond John L. Pilsworth's prominent millinery and ladies' outfitter's shop, stepladders on the pavement suggest that painters were at work on the Original Cake Shop.

A quiet Sunday morning in Parson's Street with the sun streaming across from Church Lane to illuminate a corner of the Reindeer. The bust of Shakespeare now sits above a very different Photofinish shopfront at no. 46. Down towards the Market Place Parson's Street has retained much of its character, but development in the late 1960s claimed properties on the right beyond Church Lane.

The Globe Room in the yard of the Reindeer Inn, *c*. 1900. The Reindeer is first recorded by that name in 1664 but the building dates back to the mid-sixteenth century with substantial additions in 1570 and 1624. The Globe Room was an extension of the highest quality built in 1637, incorporating excellent oak panelling and a fine plaster ceiling, and it was clearly intended to attract the most prosperous travellers. The inn later declined because it was badly placed for coaching traffic.

The Globe Room remains but the old service building of about 1600 beyond it has been removed. The Hook Norton Brewery Co. sold the Globe Room panelling, the ceiling and other fittings for £1,000 in 1912 and these items were thought to have been exported to the United States. In 1964, however, the panelling was traced to a furniture factory in Islington and it was brought back to Banbury, being restored to the Globe Room in 1981. The plaster ceiling had been stored elsewhere in London and was perhaps destroyed by bombing during the war.

Children gather outside the Original Cake Shop during celebrations for the Coronation of Edward VII, 1902. Banbury Cakes were first mentioned in 1586 and their fame spread in the eighteenth century when Betty White and her husband Jarvis owned the Original Cake Shop. The shop was taken over by Mrs E.W. Brown in 1872 and the date 1638, marking the beginning of cake making on the site, was added to the façade during a subsequent restoration of the premises.

The Plaza Indian restaurant and Fashion Fabrics now occupy the site of the Original Cake Shop. The last Banbury Cakes were baked at the shop in May 1967 and a property company submitted plans for a shopping development to include the Original Cake Shop and properties up to Church Lane. Local campaigners battled to save the building, but demolition started in April 1968 and a building preservation order came too late to save one of Banbury's most historic structures.

Window shoppers in Parson's Street, *c.* 1930. A bracketed lamp advertises the *Banbury Guardian* office at nos 51 and 52 which were home to the local newspaper from its foundation in 1838. Further up the street, beyond Lees' the tobacconist's, the Reindeer Inn is announced by a hugely projecting sign. On the left, the Original Cake Shop is followed by a group of Victorian premises.

The Reindeer's sign, now supported by a straight bracket, continues to be the main focus of attention. The redevelopment of the site between the Original Cake Shop and Church Lane is the major change, but many older properties have been retained and smartened up. On the right the former *Banbury Guardian* premises, vacated when the newspaper moved to The Green in 1976, are now occupied by Banbury Bags and Baggage and the Essential Sports Co. Brick paving enhances the pavement and extends across a 'sleeping policeman'.

Children pose outside the Corn Hill Stores on the corner of Parson's Street, *c.* 1900. Built in about 1653 in the aftermath of the Civil War, this fine building was occupied by Joseph Bush who was a grocer and tea dealer, a wine and spirit merchant and a coal factor and colliery agent.

The Corn Hill Stores were replaced by these up-to-date commercial premises in 1905. The Edwardian building, occupied for many years by Lennard's and now by Mister Minit, has many decorative features and retains attractive tiles from the original shop front. The shop next door in Cornhill was formerly the *Oxford Mail*'s Banbury office.

Cornhill, with a railway parcels van outside B.R. Morland's stationery shop, *c.* 1920. Gillett's Bank, established in 1822 and rebuilt in 1847, is behind the ornamental lamp post and the bank manager, William Charles Braithwaite (d. 1922), lived at Castle House, down to the left. The Plough pub in the bank's shadow had an off-licence window visited in the evenings by old ladies seeking medicinal gin or whisky. Next to the Plough, the impressive Vine was built as a Corn Exchange in 1857 and converted into 'a very large "barn" of a pub' in the 1880s. The goddess Ceres on the roof of the building had lost her head during a storm in December 1900!

Gillett's bank was taken over by Barclays in 1919 and the Cornhill branch closed down in the 1930s, becoming the local headquarters of the St John Ambulance Brigade for many years. The eighteenth-century Castle House survives as offices in the shadow of Banbury's multi-storey car park. Behind an over-large plane tree the Plough has gone but the frontages of the Vine and other adjoining buildings were retained during the Castle Shopping Centre development in the 1970s. Hidden by the tree, a new statue of Ceres was installed above the old Corn Exchange façade in 1983.

Market day outside the Unicorn, mid-1860s. Many Banbury buildings were destroyed during the Civil War when the Royalist-held castle was besieged in 1644 and 1646. The Unicorn, probably built in 1648, was an early and striking replacement and the building was certainly an inn by 1676. John Cheney, landlord of the Unicorn, began printing here in 1767 and Thomas Hunt, the founder of Hunt, Edmunds Brewery, started brewing on the premises in 1807. Beyond the Unicorn, Charles Pettit's drapery shop occupied the so-called Prebendal House, a building of the 1660s refronted in the eighteenth or early nineteenth century.

Three shoppers make their way towards today's market stalls outside the Unicorn. In the 1930s Kays Modern Food Stores had taken over the shop in front of the Unicorn and emblazoned their slogan 'Kays Ways Pays' across the gabled dormers. The building was eventually restored from a poor condition by the Nationwide Building Society between 1971 and 1973. Next door, the Prebendal House was given a very plain ironstone frontage during a drastic restoration in the early 1970s.

The Market Place from the Unicorn, *c.* 1878. Carriers came to Banbury on market days from every significant place within 10 miles and nearly 300 were said to attend the market in 1854. Some of their carts are visible here, and there are produce stalls outside some of the shops. Most of the activity seems to be concentrated near the Angel on the corner of Castle Street where pigs were generally sold.

Banburyshire villagers now use cars rather than carriers to do their shopping, but the Market Place itself is little changed. The façades on the left were carefully preserved in the 1970s when the Castle Shopping Centre was built. In the distance, beyond masking plane trees, the presence of a crane indicates work in progress on the Castle Quay Shopping Centre.

A dog takes the air in a quiet Market Place, early 1920s. Two youngsters try out bicycles from Curry's shop at no. 7 on the far left; further along, at nos 9–10, a huge dustpan on the wall advertises Nathan's hardware shop which has stock spilling out into the roadway. The Palace Cinema advertises a double bill and Robins' ironmonger's shop is prominent on the corner of Butcher's Row.

Except on market days, cars have taken over the Market Place, but the view is remarkably unchanged. No. 7 is now a kebab and burger restaurant and Nathan's premises are occupied by A-Plan.

The Old Gaol in the Market Place, *c.* 1910. Erected as a wool market by Banbury Corporation in 1610, this building probably became the town gaol in 1646. The Blue Coat School, founded in 1701, used the upper floor until the early nineteenth century. In 1852 the Inspector of Prisons described the gaol as the worst that he had ever seen and it was closed in 1854.

Part of the Old Gaol has survived but the Ladbroke's portion has been unsympathetically refronted and the gabled dormers have been lost. To the left, Sue Ryder's charity shop occupies the site of the Fox pub.

CHAPTER TWO

HIGH STREET &
BRIDGE STREET

A lively scene on the pavement outside the post office in High Street, 1970s. Banbury's post office was moved to this site from Parson's Street in 1849, but this very dignified neo-Georgian building was erected as the town's head post office in 1936.

The Exchange pub now occupies the former post office which closed in 1984. The countryside now seems a long way from High Street, but Arthur Jones recalled an incident here in the early 1900s when a friend's pig collapsed outside the post office on its way to Trolley's slaughterhouse in Broad Street. A slaughterman despatched the unfortunate animal on this very spot.

Children and cyclists enjoy the freedom of the High Street, 1900s. Blinds on the right protect shop displays from the afternoon sun and a lamp hangs outside the White Horse. On the corner of Calthorpe Street, H.C. Fisher ran a Bible Society Depot at 32 High Street for a few years from about 1905.

High Street today with widened pavements and necessary segregation between pedestrians and vehicles. The view towards Banbury Cross is dominated by the clock bracketed out from Anker's premises on the corner of Calthorpe Street. This was erected in 1911 by F.W. Ginger, a clockmaker, jeweller and optician, to mark the Coronation of George V.

Afghan coats and flared trousers in White Lion Walk, December 1978. The former hotel yard, with its famous wisteria on the right, led through to extensive stabling where customers during the Railway Age left their horses and carriages before catching the hotel bus to the station. Following the closure of the hotel, the yard was imaginatively transformed into a small shopping mall in 1977.

Different fashions in White Lion Walk, November 1998. The wisteria, reputedly about 240 years old, had to be carefully cradled during the creation of the shopping centre and has continued to flourish in this civilised setting. The Walk links up with Church Lane at its northern end, adding to the enjoyable network of pedestrian streets around St Mary's Church.

A cyclist wheels smartly round a distracted pedestrian outside the White Lion Hotel, 1950s. The White Lion was first recorded in 1554 and Marjory Lester recalled it as the best hotel in town, beautifully furnished with antiques and equipped with windsor chairs and pewter tankards in the bar. Managed by Jim Thewlis between 1948 and 1972, the White Lion was noted for its cuisine, but its trade subsequently declined and the hotel closed in 1975.

The building was restored in 1978 to form an attractive entrance to the White Lion Shopping Walk. The White Lion, now known as the Slurping Toad, reopened as a pub in 1995 and marks the beginning of the High Street pedestrian zone instituted in 1991. In the background, Burton's tailor's shop closed in the late 1970s and the building, now occupied by Richards Ladieswear, has lost its Burton up-stand.

Bartlett's shop at 23 High Street, *c.* 1910. Billy Bartlett was a taxidermist and he displayed eye-catching examples of his artistry both inside and outside the shop. He was also a skilled photographer and was one of the first growers of tomatoes in Banbury, raising them in a large greenhouse and selling them in his shop.

No. 23 High Street was Bartlett's angler's shop for some years before the TSB opened a new branch at nos 23 and 24 in 1977. The picture includes, on the left, a glimpse of the Victorian premises occupied by Mawle's, one of Banbury's famous ironmongery businesses until the late 1970s.

High Street from the corner of Butcher Row, November 1960. Parked cars occupy the north side of the street where H. Samuel's shop provided a public clock for passers-by. On the right, pedestrians are largely confined to a narrow pavement as they pass W.H. Robeson's tailor's shop at no. 16 and Werff Bros Ltd, ladies' outfitters at no. 15.

The paved and traffic-free street gives shoppers the chance to roam unhindered along today's High Street. Most of the buildings still reflect the transformation of central Banbury in the mid-nineteenth century but the shops are very much of the present day.

High Street, looking west past the Red Lion, 1920s. The Red Lion dated back to the late fifteenth or early sixteenth century and Marjory Lester recalled that it was always bright with tubs and hanging baskets. It was at the hub of Banbury life, a venue for auction sales, Corporation dinners and trade in corn and seeds on market days. On the right, Boots the Chemist advertised prominently at nos 79–80 and is remembered for a large flashing sign on the roof that was visible all over town.

Woolworth's acquired and demolished the Red Lion for a 3d and 6d store which opened in 1931; the firm closed its Banbury shop in the 1980s and the premises are now occupied by Mothercare and the Abbey National Bank. Nos 79–80 High Street are now more discreetly occupied by Dorothy Perkins; further up, the three-gabled property on the corner of Church Lane was replaced in about 1930 by a standard Burton's shop.

The east end of High Street, late 1930s. The view is dominated by Edward Vivers' splendid timber-framed and gabled house built in 1650; for many years, the building was occupied by Brown's Banbury Cake shop and by the ironmonger's, Neale and Perkins. The parked vehicles include a van from Colebrook's the fishmongers at no. 6, but Neale's were still defying the traffic by displaying goods in the roadway. They are remembered as selling 'everything you could imagine in the way of tools, household wares, nuts, bolts, screws and oil lamps'.

Vivers' house still graces a High Street that was pedestrianised in 1991. On the right, Levis are on special offer at the Jeans Station where Colebrook's sold fresh fish in the 1930s.

High Street from the corner of Broad Street, 1950s. A tall concrete lamp-post brings a touch of modernity to the scene and Trinder Bros at no. 84 are now offering Murphy televisions and radios. Timothy White's and Taylor's chemist's shop occupied no. 88 for many years and no. 88A was a butcher's shop, the British & Argentine Meat Co. Ltd.

Untroubled by traffic, shoppers make good use of the full width of High Street outside G.S. Clothing and Next. On the right, Thomas Cook's now offers a rather different brand of remedies at No. 88, and Marshell's newsagent's shop has taken over what became Dewhurst's.

Town Hall Buildings looking south towards Bridge Street, January 1975. Bonham's watchmaker's and jeweller's business fronted on to a street that seems never to have had an official name. In the early twentieth century it was sometimes known as Looking Glass Street because a mirror was erected at each end to help drivers to see oncoming hazards.

The homely jumble of buildings behind the Town Hall was demolished in 1977 and a smart modern branch of the NatWest bank took their place. 'Looking Glass Street' is now traffic-free.

The old and the new in Bridge Street, June 1967. Special offers attract a throng of shoppers and their cars to a brash new Fine Fare supermarket on the site of the Catherine Wheel pub. To the right, the Baptist church had also been built on the site of an old inn, the Altarstone, in 1841. The fine Ionic portico originally had three pairs of columns and two entrance doors, but the columns were rearranged in 1903 to provide a central entrance.

Fine Fare expanded into the former Baptist church in about 1972 but the portico was retained, looking uncomfortably like a film set creation. The premises are now separate again with Superdrug in the original supermarket and Bewise behind the portico. Parked cars have been pushed back a little by shrub and tree planting. Part of Barclays Bank, a dignified 1930s building, is visible to the right.

High Street from the Town Hall, 1956. The traffic seems light but parked cars occupy all the available space at the roadside. Beyond the Town Hall, commercial premises included Leach's sweet shop and the half-timbered building occupied for many years by the Refuge Assurance Co. Ltd.

Brick paving, Victorian-style street furniture and an extraordinary Tardis-like public toilet are elements of the High Street pedestrianisation completed in 1991. The plane trees have flourished and motorists now have to Pay and Display for convenient parking spaces in Bridge Street.

Market day in Bridge Street or Cow Fair, early 1920s. A lively scene outside the Town Hall when cattle were still being penned along both sides of the street; local lads could hope to earn 6*d* by 'cow bunting', that is, by looking after cattle at the market and then driving them to their new owner's field. A motorist is trying an adventurous route through the crowd and a local bus awaits passengers beside the lamp-post.

Cattle sales by auction were transferred to the new Grimsbury premises of Midland Marts Ltd in 1925; private sales followed in 1931, leaving Bridge Street a cleaner and, for a time, quieter thoroughfare. Traffic and parked cars gradually filled the vacuum and the area outside the Town Hall became a very basic bus station until the new Castle Street bus station opened in 1968. Bridge Street is currently undergoing another massive change as the Castle Quay Shopping Centre is built on the north side.

Banbury Town Hall from Cow Fair, *c.* 1880. The Town Hall, designed by the Oxford architect Edward Bruton, and built in 1854, dominates a market day scene of cattle and parked carriers' carts. The building was partly funded by the town's MP Henry Tancred, and by Lord Saye and Sele. A dinner and a soirée for 600 people were held to mark its completion in October 1854, but it was another six years before the clock was installed. The Corporation's fire escape ladder can be seen against the Town Hall wall next to the men's urinal. Lamprey's seed merchant's shop is visible away to the right at 34 Bridge Street.

Plane trees were planted in Bridge Street in the 1890s and they have flourished in the urban environment. They provide welcome shade in summer but have obscured much of the townscape. The Town Hall is now only glimpsed from this spot but preserved advertisements are visible on Lamprey's old shop, which closed in 1980 and is now a branch of the Halifax.

The north side of Bridge Street on a peaceful afternoon, 1920s. H.O. White's corn, seed and coal merchant's business occupied no. 43, the gabled building on the corner, with Atkins & Co.'s oil cake business to the left on the corner of Mill Lane; the entrance to Banbury Wharf is just visible on the other side of Mill Lane. Down Bridge Street, the tall building with a prominent cornice was the Cadbury Memorial Hall, built in 1876 as a Temperance Hall and British Workman; its facilities included hot and cold baths. With adjoining buildings, it later became the Waverley Temperance Hotel and then the Blue Bird Commercial and Temperance Hotel. Part of the building was used as a Labour Exchange for men between the wars.

Two plane trees remain, but the north side of Bridge Street was demolished in 1998 for the Castle Quay Shopping Centre. The façade of the Cadbury Memorial Hall was retained and will keep alive local memories of the old Blue Bird hotel and the building's founder, James Cadbury, a local Quaker and uncle of George Cadbury, founder of the Bournville factory. Archaeological excavations on the site confirmed that there were properties on the Bridge Street frontage in medieval times.

CHAPTER THREE

CASTLE STREET TO
SOUTHAM ROAD

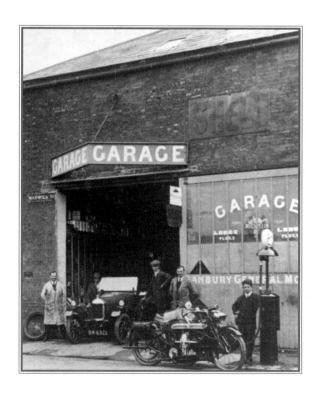

Factory Street, looking east from Castle Street North, April 1969. Factory Street took its name from Cobb's horse girth factory between the Oxford Canal and the river Cherwell. It extended from a covered passage beside the Plough on Cornhill to a drawbridge over the canal and was home to Mold's, Banbury's only tripe and cow heel shop.

The Castle Shopping Centre obliterated Factory Street in the 1970s but this shopping mall is on the same alignment. Built at a cost of £4 million, the development provided twenty-eight shop units behind the Market Place and included the International Supermarket and premises for Boots and W.H. Smith. The shopping centre was in use by July 1977 but the official opening by the Duke of Gloucester took place on 3 May 1978.

Compton Street, looking south from Castle Street East, May 1969. This cul-de-sac of twenty houses was built in the 1870s and 1880s. Cicely Bailey recalled the properties as 'very nice, small and clean, the roadway being stony, as the council never "made it up"'.

Banbury Castle was slighted after the Civil War and the north side of the Castle Shopping Centre, occupying the site of Compton Street, provides a 1970s interpretation of the castle complete with a 'dry moat' and 'battlements'. Partially obscured by shrubs, an entrance door from the moat provides pedestrian access to the centre.

Castle Street East, looking down towards the Castle Wharf, July 1964. This was a largely residential street of two- and three-storey brick houses built in the mid- to late nineteenth century. There were just two shops in the street, a 'front room' sweet shop and Croxton's bakery where people had their Sunday dinners cooked. The better houses had cold running water but no bathrooms or hot water on tap.

Castle Street was extended down to Bridge Street in the 1960s as part of the bus station development. Every house has gone, those on the right replaced by the appropriately defensive-looking Castle Shopping Centre built between 1976 and 1977. Hoardings on the left anticipate the development of the Castle Quay Shopping Centre which will soon transform this scene beyond all recognition.

The exit from Castle Street West to North Bar and Southam Road, *c.* 1960. Narrowing to about 8 ft at the junction, the road was a considerable traffic hazard and passing vehicles often scraped the side wall of the Three Pigeons pub as they squeezed through the gap. In the 1920s Hayden's smithy flourished on the left at the back of the Three Horseshoes and provided exciting sights and sounds for children on their way into town.

The Three Pigeons has been protected by a wide pavement since the demolition of the Three Horseshoes and adjoining buildings blasted open the west end of Castle Street in the 1960s. The clearance of the corner of North Bar and Warwick Road adds to the sense of desolation.

Southam Road from North Bar, 1939. The mid-nineteenth century Three Horseshoes pub obscures the entrance to Castle Street and the Three Pigeons beyond it. More nineteenth-century houses are followed by the gables of St Mary's Church of England School, rebuilt in 1900 on the site of Banbury National School (1817). Children from Banbury Workhouse attended St Mary's School, being marched every day down Warwick Road by a burly ex-Regimental Sergeant Major 'with a big voice, and useful walking cane'.

Demolition of the Three Horseshoes has exposed the Three Pigeons pub to view. It is an attractive ironstone building with a thatched roof and dates from the seventeenth century; in the early 1800s it was used for meetings of the Hundreds of Banbury Manorial Court. Its semi-subterranean appearance is the result of the realignment of North Bar by the Banbury Paving and Lighting Commissioners in about 1826.

Banbury General Motor Garage in Warwick Road, early 1920s. The garage was established in part of the old Austin's brewery behind North Bar in about 1920 and prospered in this key position near the junction of the Warwick and Southam roads.

The garage closed in the early 1970s and the site, including surviving parts of Austin's brewery, was cleared in 1993 in readiness for the building of a new courthouse. For the moment, the corner of North Bar and Warwick Road is entirely given over to car parking.

Southam Road looking south towards St Mary's Church, February 1975. These two- and three-storey brick houses extended the built-up area of Banbury northwards in the 1870s and housed relatively prosperous families. At the back, the properties overlooked an open area known as the Marches where boys from the nearby St Mary's School settled their differences.

Nos 18–20 Southam Road survive beside the school but other properties have given way to a prestigious new development called The Village, which makes more intensive use of the site.

The steelwork for Bird's new coffee plant rears above the Banbury landscape, 1964. The Northern Aluminium Company's premises were a massive development in the 1930s but they were comparatively hidden from the town; the same could certainly not be said for Bird's custard factory which relocated from central Birmingham with the encouragement of Banbury Borough Council.

Kraft Jacobs Suchard's factory in Southam Road. Bird's offices moved to Banbury in October 1964 but production only began in the autumn of 1966. The buildings have been a Banbury landmark for travellers by road and rail ever since and the aroma of coffee drifts temptingly across the neighbourhood. Bird's name was lost to General Foods and the Kraft Jacobs Suchard group was the product of another merger in 1989.

The General Foods factory from the Oxford Canal at Grimsbury Wharf, September 1981. The drawbridge carried traffic from Southam Road across the canal to the waterworks at Grimsbury.

The building of Hennef Way in 1990–1 required the Oxford Canal to be diverted and the stub of the old waterway is visible at the foot of the road embankment. The expanded General Foods factory, now part of the Kraft Jacobs Suchard group, stands beyond a large Citroën garage in a totally changed Southam Road.

Flooding on the Southam Road near the Ironstone Railway bridge, March 1947. The Ironstone Railway was built in 1917–18 for the Oxfordshire Ironstone Co. Ltd, and locals sometimes called it the German Railway because it was built with the help of 250 German prisoners of war housed in Banbury Workhouse. Beyond the bridge and the hidden Northern Aluminium Company works, Southam Road can be seen curving away up Hardwick Hill.

A very much wider Southam Road now passes an overgrown railway embankment on the left. The Ironstone Railway closed on 30 September 1967 with the run-down of the local quarrying industry. The Southam Road railway bridge was demolished in June 1969.

The Alcan factory from the Oxford Canal, 1950s. The horse-drawn narrowboat and the steam locomotive on the Oxfordshire Ironstone Railway already seem like survivors from another era, apparently out of step with the huge bulk of the aluminium factory and the marching electricity pylons.

Despite the looming presence of the Alcan works there is still a rural feel to the Oxford Canal at this point as it turns sharply away from Southam Road. Trees have grown out of the hedgerow beside the towpath and the old Ironstone Railway embankment is overgrown, softening the landscape; most surprisingly perhaps, the pylons have gone.

The Northern Aluminium Company's works, with bikes and works buses occupying the foreground, 1952. The company's first rolling mill began commercial production in November 1931 and the number of employees rose from an initial 200 to 4,000 during the Second World War when 'The Alley' was producing aluminium for Spitfires and Bailey Bridges. Many wartime employees were women who were brought in by bus from villages around Banbury and often nodded off on the way home after long, arduous shifts.

Northern Aluminium became Alcan in 1960 and most of the firm's employees now arrive by car rather than by bike or bus. Alcan's sports centre at the far end of the car park was demolished in about 1995, revealing views of Hardwick Hill. During the war a dummy aluminium factory of wood and canvas was built over the hill to confuse enemy bombers.

CHAPTER FOUR

OLD TOWN HALL WHARF
TO CALTHORPE MANOR

Old Town Hall Wharf in Lower Cherwell Street, February 1975. The building in the background with the base of a cupola on the roof was built as Banbury's Town Hall in 1800. It originally stood outside the Unicorn in the Market Place and was relocated to this canal-side wharf as a warehouse in 1860 after its Victorian successor had been completed. Until recently Chapman's of Banbury used it for storage.

The old Town Hall survives, sandwiched between premises occupied by King Lifting and Central Tyres. Paint has obliterated the bold advertisements for Palmer & Son, one of the many coal merchants that were formerly located beside the Oxford Canal.

The Three Tuns pub in Cherwell Street, when the area was being cleared in the 1970s. Almost inevitably, perhaps, the Three Tuns was a Hunt, Edmunds pub and it was first recorded in about 1858. Derek John Waters was the landlord for many years from 1953.

Pints of beer have given way to litres of petrol in modern Cherwell Street. The tall brick office building in the background was originally the headquarters of Crest Hotels Europe.

Workmen board up condemned houses in Lower Windsor Street, October 1962. A mix of two- and three-storey houses, most of these mid-nineteenth-century properties still lacked bathrooms and inside toilets. Their occupants were being re-housed to new semi-detached council houses on Banbury's suburban estates.

Grass and trees fill the space between a widened Windsor Street and the industrial estate in Lower Cherwell Street.

Upper Windsor Street, looking north towards Windsor Terrace, August 1971. The two- and three-storey brick houses, with small front gardens, were built in about 1845.

The houses are gone but an unkempt hedge hiding a car park echoes the line of their boundary fences. Beyond Windsor Terrace, the Blarney Stone pub was first recorded as the Mechanics Arms in about 1869 and was later known as the Britannia. Samuelson's Upper Works, on the site of Gardner's original foundry, lay just beyond the pub.

The east side of Upper Windsor Street looking south from Canal Street, February 1975. Two-storey brick houses, ornamented only by decorative plaster lintels above doors and windows, these properties were built to house a growing population in the 1840s. Flooding was always a problem in these low-lying streets after heavy storms.

A much widened Windsor Street became part of Banbury's inner relief road in 1991, and these parked cars occupy the back gardens of the demolished Victorian houses.

Henry Stone & Son Ltd's furniture factory on the corner of Gatteridge Street and Upper Windsor Street, 1970s. Built in 1883, these premises marked part of the rapid expansion of a business developed by Henry Stone, a Banbury bookseller, who began to manufacture a patented letter filing box in 1871. He diversified into cabinet making and the firm was later noted for its Fyne Ladye of Banbury quality furniture.

Stone's furniture business collapsed in 1977 and the site is now occupied by the Swan Industrial Estate. Upper Windsor Street now continues up the hill past Swan Close Road to Oxford Road as part of Banbury's inner relief road.

Henry Stone & Son's derelict Britannia Road premises awaiting a new use in the 1980s. These substantial buildings, erected in the 1900s, provided extra space for the furniture business and for box making. Despite the diversification of a business that included a printing works in Swan Close Road by 1915, local people always referred to Stone's as the 'box factory'.

Stone's buildings were destroyed by fire and have been replaced by the three-storeyed Kimberley Villas. Brick pilasters and elliptical arches above doors and windows provide faint echoes of the past. Albert Kimberley was a major brickmaker and builder in Victorian Banbury with a brickworks in Broughton Road and his builder's yard in Britannia Road.

The west side of Britannia Road, 1970s. The street was laid out in the 1850s as the rapid expansion of Samuelson's Britannia Works generated a demand for new housing. These properties backed on to Braggins' timber yard which was noted for its oak field gates and wheelbarrows. Local people queued at the gates to buy cheap firewood on Saturday mornings.

Britannia Road today, with Samuelson Court, a block of eighty flats that extends round into Grove Street and Gatteridge Street. Set back from the pavement, the block exposes the side wall of the former Britannia Road Infants' School.

Children pose for a final photograph outside Britannia Road Infants' School on the day that the school closed, 25 May 1983. Formerly known as Cherwell British Schools, the school was built in 1861 at the expense of Bernhard Samuelson, owner of the nearby Britannia Works. The firm's Mutual Instruction & Recreation Society used the building for recreational purposes and Samuelson provided employees with a slipper bath and a library in adjoining buildings.

The building found a new use as Banbury Day Centre for the elderly in 1984 and maintains a welcome degree of continuity in a much-altered area. This cheerful group of people enjoying the facilities includes, fifth from left, Mrs Waine, who was a pupil at the school back in 1932.

The last surviving house in Spring Cottages, no. 20, 1970. Spring Cottages was a long row of three-storey brick houses built by 1847. It was approached from Britannia Road and backed on to Jubilee Terrace and premises occupied by Friswell's, the iron merchants.

Amos Court now occupies the site of Spring Cottages and Jubilee Court fronts on to nearby George Street.

The massive malthouse of Hunt, Edmunds brewery, viewed from George Street, 1973. Thomas Hunt established a brewery at the Unicorn in Market Place in 1807 and moved to Bridge Street in 1847. William Edmunds was taken into partnership in 1850 and this malthouse, built by Albert Kimberley of Banbury in 1866, was part of a substantial enlargement of the brewery.

Brewing at Hunt, Edmunds brewery ceased in 1967 and the site was cleared in 1974. The Cherwell Shopping Centre was built on the land behind Bridge Street in 1977–78; towards George Street, the brewery site now provides car parking and an area of open space.

Christ Church from the north-west, 1920s. The parish of South Banbury was created in 1846 to serve the growing population in the Cherwell Meadows; churchmen also felt that an anglican presence was needed to counter papal aggression and the growth of non-conformity. Christ Church was designed by Benjamin Ferrey and built between 1851 and 1852; Samuel Wilberforce, the Bishop of Oxford, consecrated the church on 19 February 1853. Ferrey's design envisaged a tower and spire but only the tower was added in 1880.

Jubilee Court on the corner of Broad Street and George Street. Described in 1939 as 'extremely poor and very exacting', South Banbury parish was finally merged with St Mary's in 1967 and Christ Church closed. The building was demolished in 1970 and Jubilee Court now stands on the site. To the right, the Victorian 18 Broad Street has survived this massive change.

The old Coachsmith's Arms pub on the corner of Broad Street and Fish Street, *c.* 1900. Behind the throng of children eager to appear in the photograph, a passage led through to Church Court which J.L. Langley recalled as having 'a most unsavoury reputation'. Down Fish Street, the modern George Street, a sign announces premises used by C. Lampitt & Co.'s Christ Church engineering works.

Banbury Co-operative Society acquired the corner site and these distinctive premises, designed by A.E. Allen, were opened in August 1908. Described as 'a working man's palace in a working man's district', they provided space for the firm's grocery and tailoring departments and featured a cash railway in both shops. The corner turret boasted the town's first electric clock. Classical Lighting of Banbury now makes good use of the shop, which retains its original tiled shop front.

Broad Street and the Grand Cinema, October 1964. The first Grand Cinema opened here in 1911 and Arthur Jones recalled massive queues extending round into George Street for some of the early mystery serials that were shown in weekly episodes. The new cinema erected in 1935 was described as being modern with 'grace and dignity in its proportions, its main lines being emphasised by the use of red and green neon lights'. The Co-op Arcade, built opposite in 1934, is remembered by Cicely Bailey as a wonderful shop, well stocked with useful goods at affordable prices; its attractions included the first public lift in Banbury and a Cosy Café for Dainty Teas on the first floor.

Today's pedestrianised Broad Street, where the former Banbury Co-operative Society Arcade is now occupied by the stationery shop Paperways, and an Argos showroom. The Grand Cinema became part of the ABC chain of cinemas in 1938, and in November 1939 its steel inner roof was advertised as a safety feature in the event of an air raid. Like so many cinemas the Grand lost custom in the 1960s and it closed with a final performance of *Where were you when the lights went out?* on 14 December 1968. The building reopened as a bingo hall in January 1969.

Christ Church Parish Hall on the corner of Broad Street and Newland Place, January 1975. A short cul-de-sac, Newland Place was laid out in 1870 on part of the Calthorpe House estate and provided room for nineteen terraced houses; it was originally known as Grove Place.

The Victorian parish hall has been restored and effectively converted into retail units with small shopfronts in place of the ground floor windows. Newland Place is still intact and its television aerials compete with the distant tower of St Mary's Church.

Girls from Dashwood Road School pose in the school playground, *c.* 1910. The Wesleyans built the school in 1901–2 to remedy the lack of school places in Banbury and ran it on undenominational lines. Following the 1902 Education Act, Banbury Borough Council became an elementary education authority and took over the management of the school.

Members of today's Year 2 with their teacher, Rebecca Everall, in the playground of Dashwood County Primary School. Oxfordshire County Council assumed responsibility for Banbury's primary schools in 1944.

All eyes turn to watch a car emerge from the Red Lion Tap in Fish Street, the modern George Street, *c.* 1910. On the right, Goodway's Coach Works occupied premises on the corner of Pepper Alley; Tom Goodway recalled how they had to place vehicles on planks across the street and use a hand-operated pulley to haul them up to the first-floor workshop where the man is standing. The Red Lion Tap was built behind the Red Lion in 1907 and reflected the then fashionable Arts and Crafts movement with its pebble-dashed walls and deep eaves. Further up, the four-storey warehouse with hoists was used by Mawle's the ironmongers until the 1970s.

George Street, looking past Pepper Alley. Goodway's diversified into car painting and spraying, building repair and decorating and the firm lasted until 1984 when Tom Goodway retired. The attractive Red Lion Tap was demolished in 1977 for an extension to Woolworth's.

A Daimler purrs up a busy George Street, April 1962. The Wheatsheaf pub, a stone building dating perhaps from the seventeenth century, sits a little uneasily beside the Salvation Army 'fortress' or Citadel built in 1890 at a cost of £1,400. Further down, at no. 64, 'Cooked Meats' were on sale at the North Oxfordshire Pork & Bacon Supply shop. On the left, artists' materials were being sold by Stella, a china dealer at 3 George Street.

The Wheatsheaf still flourishes and the Salvation Army, which was considering a new citadel in 1978, is still based in George Street. Further down, most old properties have gone, leaving only fading memories of Jimmy Soden the chimney sweep at no. 54 and John Butters' pawnshop, known affectionately as 'Uncle's', round the corner in Broad Street.

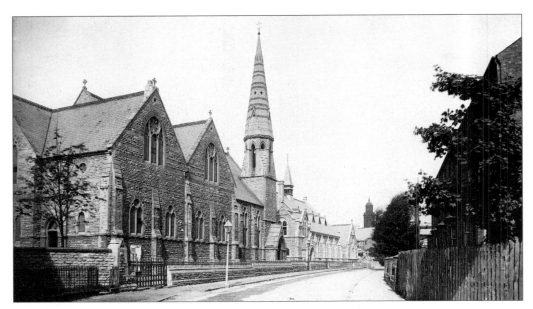

The Wesleyan Methodist Church and Sunday Schools in Marlborough Road, probably 1880s. The buildings demonstrate the size and the wealth of the Methodist community in Victorian Banbury. The church was designed by George Woodhouse and built at a cost of £6,800 between 1864 and 1865; a special fund was needed to build the spire because many non-conformists were hostile to spires as symbols of the Established Church.

Marlborough Road Methodist Church from the junction with Marlborough Place and Albert Street. The church, minus a few gable end crosses, is still a powerful physical presence in central Banbury. A few cars have invaded the church precincts and the railings on the front wall have gone, probably to wartime salvage.

The men who built the Marlborough Road Methodist Sunday School in 1882. William Mewburn, a stockbroker who settled at Wykham Park in 1865, provided £2,000 towards the cost of this extensive building.

A fragment of stone wall on the left is the sole reminder of the old Sunday School, demolished in 1986. Where children once went in search of religious instruction, motorists now look for parking spaces in the Marlborough Road Car Park.

Looking from Marlborough Road into High Street, April 1910. Marlborough Road was laid out in 1863 on a portion of the Calthorpe Estate and one property was acquired to provide a very narrow exit to High Street; an early cautionary sign warns road users to 'Drive Slowly'.

Premises alongside 29 High Street were shaved off to widen the exit from Marlborough Road and the retaining wall of Marlborough Road Car Park is visible to the left. The bland 1960s replacement for the White Horse pub stands on the far side of High Street, but on the right-hand corner of Marlborough Road the side elevation of 27 High Street, S.H. Jones' wine merchant's, maintains a strong link with the past.

The lively community of Calthorpe Street celebrates VE (Victory in Europe) Day, May 1945. Calthorpe Street boasted three pubs, the Plough, the Globe and the Black Swan, and a huge range of trades from banana ripener to whitesmith; Cheney's printing works was located there from 1896 and W.G. Cheney is standing in the centre of the group wearing a white linen jacket.

Picturesque but neglected Calthorpe Street has almost entirely gone and its community with it. Cheney's gave way to the Marlborough Road Car Park and a Sainsbury's supermarket in 1986; Sainsbury's moved on to Oxford Road in 1994 and their old store is now occupied by Richard Kimbell's and T.K. Maxx. Higham's Solid Fuels building is the last remnant of Calthorpe Gardens, a vanished cul-de-sac built in the 1870s. Further on, the removal of Hyde's furniture factory has revealed St John's Roman Catholic Church, built in 1838.

Calthorpe Manor from the north-west, a drawing by Edward Bruton dating from 1850. The north range and ornate entrance porch were built, perhaps for the Danvers family, in the late sixteenth or early seventeenth century, but parts of the house may be a hundred years older. The house was substantially remodelled in Gothic style in the eighteenth and early nineteenth centuries and its grounds extended to High Street, Broad Street and St John's Road. The lake to the north of the house 'was often used for boating, or fishing, or skating, and proved a great source of pleasure to the family at all seasons of the year'.

Calthorpe Manor from the roof of Richard Kimbell's furniture store. A series of land sales beginning in 1833 robbed the house of its extensive grounds and a firm of carriage proprietors drained the lake and converted the site into business premises in about 1903. From 1875 William Shilson used part of the house for storing wool and he added large brick warehouses that later became part of Hyde's furniture factory. Having survived so many indignities and even the threat of demolition in 1977, Calthorpe Manor is now divided into flats; the remains of the lake caused brief consternation when Sainsbury's supermarket was built nearby in the 1980s.

CHAPTER FIVE

South Bar to Easington

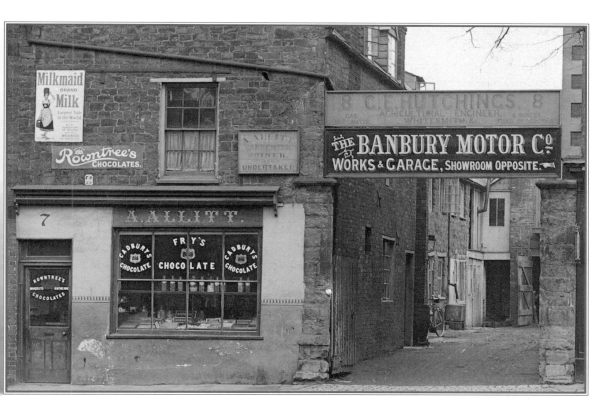

South Bar from the tower of St Mary's Church, looking south-west towards the Bloxham road, 1890s. A few people go about their business and a horse and cart pursues a leisurely course into High Street. The distinctive stuccoed Gothic houses in Crouch Street, built in about 1835, are visible on the right. At this time development ended at Beargarden Road and there were still fields on either side of Bloxham Road.

Winter gives a clearer view of both older properties and newer office developments in and behind South Bar. Banbury Cross, without its railings since 1927, remains the focal point for a much-enlarged town and only the growth of trees masks the twentieth-century expansion of Banbury across Bloxham Road and into Easington. As before, there is little sense of bustle in the streets below but the parked cars stretching away up South Bar demonstrate Banbury's daily appeal to shoppers and commuters.

The Swan pub at 3 South Bar when the landlord was G.E. Davis, *c.* 1900. Henry Wright was the Swan's first recorded landlord in 1545 and the present stone building with mullioned windows and gabled attic dormers dates from the mid-seventeenth century. Away to the right, the lamplighter is up his ladder attending to one of the Borough's gas lamps.

The Swan today with plaster removed to show the building's ironstone construction. South Bar now provides convenient car parking space and the little gas lamp, providing a pool of light on the pavement, has been replaced by a huge electric lighting column casting its glow across the whole street.

Nos. 7–9 South Bar, *c*. 1910. Allitt's shop occupied the surviving part of the old Banbury workhouse which moved to this spot from Scalding Lane, the modern George Street, in 1707; the main workhouse buildings were on the site of Miss Wright's dyer's shop at no. 9. Premises in the yard were shared by a traditional agricultural engineer, G.E. Hutchings, and by a new business, Banbury Motor Company, established by two ex-cavalry officers, Captain Gooch and Captain Tarrant, in 1907. The company's showroom was on the corner of Horse Fair and West Bar.

The frontage of 7 South Bar is still recognisable behind modern windows and the Bamboo Garden's shopfront. Banbury Motor Company went on to become the Pytchley Garage and then the County Garages. Their premises here were destroyed by fire in 1931 and no. 8 is now the South Bar Snooker Club. Changing fashion has led to the disguising of old brickwork at no. 6 and no. 9.

A small dog controls the approach to South Bar, *c.* 1910. South Bar became magnificently formal in the 1820s and 1830s as the Banbury Paving and Lighting Commissioners realigned the road and created a regular footpath on the west side. They also planted trees in an attempt to beautify the street in 1826, but vandals made short work of them; the lime trees visible now were planted in 1885.

Like St Giles' in Oxford, tree-lined South Bar has proved attractive for car parking. Despite the removal of much through traffic by the opening of the M40 in 1991, the road is still well used by local traffic and is no place for idle loitering. On the left, South Bar House replaced nos 28–34 in 1978.

South Bar near the junction of Bloxham Road, 1968. The town's South Bar or gate stood here from the thirteenth century until 1785 when William Judd, a local carrier, obtained permission to demolish it as an obstruction to traffic; his commemorative monument was removed in 1843 because it had become a magnet for layabouts. The Classical-style terraced houses opposite were built in about 1835 and, to their left, the Case is Altered pub, formerly the Weavers' Arms, dated back to the seventeenth century.

The Case is Altered and 28–34 South Bar were demolished in 1973 and Alcan House, offices for Alcan Aluminium UK, occupied the site in 1978. The block now has other occupiers and has been renamed South Bar House. In the foreground, a surviving K6 telephone box maintains a tiny amount of continuity.

Milton Street, looking towards Beargarden Road, January 1975. This little brick terrace was built in the 1880s off New Road which, in spite of its name, is part of an ancient lane leading from South Bar to West or Sugarford Bar. Beargarden Road is named after an old earthwork near the junction with Bloxham Road; a semi-circular hollow cut into the hill, it provided two terraces for spectators and an arena separated from the terraces by a ditch. Another less interesting theory is that the earthwork was simply an old quarry.

A porch here and there and the odd rendered façade mark the passage of time in Milton Street; wheeliebins have also made an appearance beside the unmade-up pathway. The character of the street remains intact, however, and, with the clearance of much nineteenth-century housing in central Banbury, it is now something of a rarity.

Oxford Road looking down towards South Bar, *c.* 1930. The embanked pavement graphically illustrates how much the road was lowered in 1839 to create a steadier slope for horse-drawn vehicles. The grand villas opposite were built on part of the Calthorpe estate in the 1840s; lower down, a few older houses near the Bloxham turn stand near the site of St John's Hospital which flourished between the early thirteenth century and 1549.

On a busy main road there is a surprising degree of continuity, but tall lamp-posts are an obvious contemporary feature. Iron boundary fences have gone, probably to wartime salvage, and extra rooms have been slotted into the attic floors of nos 29 and 31. Windows have been replaced here and there and a balcony above the porch at no. 29 has been removed.

The Horton Infirmary in Oxford Road as depicted by its architect, Charles Driver, *c.* 1872. Miss Mary Jane Horton of Middleton Cheney (d. 1869) left money for the building of a hospital and this Gothic-style structure was opened in July 1872. It originally provided wards for six men and six women in the single-storey wings, with an operating theatre and staff accommodation in the two-storey central block.

Shorn of much of its Gothic detailing and with modern additions, the old part of the Horton now accommodates the outpatients' department, the pharmacy and personnel offices. The infirmary was renamed Horton General Hospital in 1927 and, having become part of the Oxford Radcliffe Hospitals Trust in 1998, it is now known simply as The Horton. Additions have included a children's ward in 1897, a maternity unit in 1961 and a new accident and emergency unit in 1989; in place of the original 12 beds, there are now 200.

Springfield Avenue, 1970. These groups of terraced houses, set back behind tree-lined grass verges and hedged front gardens, form part of the Easington estate. Built on fields that had been part of Easington Farm, this estate of 361 houses was Banbury Corporation's first response to the Housing Act of 1919.

Springfield Avenue has changed to accommodate rising levels of car ownership and increasing traffic levels. Road widening has pared back the grass verges and led to the removal of some trees. At the same time, hedges have begun to make way for car parking in front gardens.

At home; a corner of the kitchen in 107 Springfield Avenue, 1940s. A gas cooker with four rings, oven and grill has pride of place while kitchen utensils and tea towels hang from painted brick walls. It was scarcely luxurious, but in central Banbury many households still had to have their Sunday dinners cooked by the local baker because they had inadequate cooking facilities.

The same corner today with central heating radiator, microwave oven and built-in kitchen units; cupboards and ornaments hang from wood-panelled walls. Every change bears mute witness to the growth in domestic comfort since the war.

Looking down into Banbury from the Bloxham road near Springfields, *c.* 1910. From this point a footpath led down past Berrymoor Farm to join Beargarden Road at its junction with West Bar. The house, Springfields, was built in the 1870s for John Vanner, a wealthy London businessman who was a Methodist and a friend of William Mewburn at Wykham Park.

Church View retains a distant view of the tower of St Mary's Church but the old footpath has vanished under development since the 1950s, recalled only by the curious little path that leads from Bloxham Road to Brenda Close. Below Church View, Queens Way was laid out in the mid-1950s as a dual carriageway linking Bloxham Road and Broughton Road.

CHAPTER SIX

NEITHROP & RUSCOTE

Children have fun in the paddling pool in People's Park, 1967. People's Park was the result of a legacy to Banbury Corporation by George Ball, a local chemist; a portion opened in June 1912 and the rest in 1919 when the official opening formed part of the Peace celebrations at the end of the First World War. In the early days old school desks served as seats and small children could almost get lost in grass that was mown only by sheep. A bandstand was built in 1931 and the paddling pool and playground were among many improvements made at that time.

Two youngsters enjoy the climbing frame erected on the site of the paddling pool. The bandstand has gone and costs have been cut but People's Park is still a welcoming place, bright with blossom and flowers in the spring and summer.

Park Road looking towards Bath Road from the corner of Queen Street, February 1975. An attractive terrace of three-storey brick houses built in the 1870s, its occupants in 1881 included James John Day, a watchmaker, at no. 4 and Thomas Knight, the town missionary, at no. 8. The land opposite remained undeveloped until the 1930s.

Parking restrictions are now a fact of life in Park Road but the houses are little changed. Some modern shutters have been removed and, further down the street, rampant creepers on front walls recapture the spirit of a Victorian suburb.

Warwick Road, showing the Crown Inn and a pedestrian walking past the former Eagle pub, February 1975. The three-storey brick houses next to the Eagle, 70/76 Warwick Road, were among many such properties built in fast-growing Neithrop during the first half of the nineteenth century. These two pubs would have been major beneficiaries from the increasing population.

All the Warwick Road properties east of Foundry Street have been cleared and the site landscaped to improve the setting for the old people's housing in the background. The side elevation of 78 Warwick Road on the corner of Foundry Street provides the only link with the past.

Traffic splashes through floods outside Young's garage in Warwick Road, 1960s. The incident recalls complaints in 1850 about inadequate storm water drainage and consequent flooding in a street that was formerly called Water Lane. Springs of water ran so close to the surface that cellars filled with stagnant water and families living above them were liable to what was sometimes described as Banbury fever.

Young's Garage flourished on this site from the 1920s until the mid-1970s but Bennett's Family Furnishing store now uses this prominent building on the corner of Warwick Road and Bath Road.

The Vulcan Arms in Foundry Street, March 1965. Named after the nearby Vulcan Foundry and built in about 1840, the pub had an appropriate inn sign showing a blacksmith hammering on an anvil. According to a former licensee, Sid Chown, the local magistrates had refused to accept an alternative sign showing a naked lady reclining on the bed while Vulcan, her lover, climbed out of the window and her husband hammered on the door.

The Vulcan pub and adjoining buildings were swept away in the late 1970s and the Orchard Surgery and Health Centre now backs on to Foundry Street.

The creeper-clad Orchard House, Neithrop, *c.* 1900. Built in the late sixteenth or early seventeenth century, Orchard House was at least a superior farmhouse in origin. Its status was seriously compromised in Victorian times when Lampitt & Co.'s Vulcan Foundry was built on to the back of the building. In 1850 the house was occupied by William Gregory, a Unitarian gardener and seedsman who was at one time a tobacco pipe maker.

With the foundry buildings removed, Orchard House has found a new use at the centre of a surgery and health centre complex. The ironstone building, now cleared of creeper, has been carefully restored; significant changes include the matching chimney-stacks and a gabled dormer in the Stonesfield slate roof.

The butcher, Leslie Holland, stands proudly in his shop doorway at 80 Warwick Road in 1937; the lad on the right is Laurence Waters senior, his stepson. Holland's shop was in business from about 1930 to 1971.

Laurence Waters returns to his old stamping ground, now the tiled façade of the A1 Chinese restaurant, after sixty-two years.

Eastbound traffic is diverted away up Neithrop Avenue as storm water drainage work reduces Warwick Road to single lane traffic, 1960s. The bell-cote of St Paul's Church, built in 1853, rears up behind the white painted house on the left of the picture and St Mary's Church tower is prominent in the distance. On the right, Lyon's Maid ice cream was on sale at Prescott's grocery shop at 87 Warwick Road.

Prescott's shop is now Hairways but Warwick Road has changed little at this point and the two churches still punctuate the skyline. The growth of trees in front of St Paul's Church obscures a substantial garage further down and demolition has left a gap in Warwick Road opposite People's Park.

Rag Row in Warwick Road, *c.* 1890. This early nineteenth-century terrace of ten brick houses with thatched roofs was built on the corner of Union Street. Each house was apparently quite spacious, but by the late 1840s the row had an unsavoury reputation; one property used as a lodging house had no fewer than fifteen inhabitants. At this time a single privy in a yard at one end of the terrace served all the houses and was only emptied once a year.

Rag Row was slightly improved by the addition of three extra privies in 1849, but it was demolished in about 1900, an early instance of slum clearance. Between the wars 89/97 Warwick Road were built on the site, providing comfortable semi-detached houses with front flower gardens and unusual porches.

Boxhedge Square, February 1975. This area was known as Townsend Square in 1850 and the group of nineteenth-century houses on the right included a pub, the Millwright's Arms. A pair of houses called Rock Pleasant occupied part of the grassy space and the roadway until they were claimed by slum clearance. Their removal revealed older ironstone cottages in Boxhedge Road.

Yule Court now occupies the site and, being set further back from the road, it exposes to view 4 Boxhedge Road, a thatched ironstone house dating from the seventeenth century.

Boxhedge Road and Neithrop Methodist Mission Hall, February 1975. After co-operating with other non-conformist denominations to build the mission hall in Warwick Road in 1873, the Wesleyan Methodists erected this brick mission hall in 1887–8 in the poor Boxhedge area. Some old cottages at the entrance to Bolton's Lane were cleared away to form the site and the foundation stones of the building were laid by M. Mewburn, R.C. Waterfield, B. Smart and Mrs. R. Edmunds.

The red-brick Victorian Mission Hall still flourishes beside the golden ironstone of 18–19 Boxhedge Road, two seventeenth-century houses which were occupied as four dwellings in 1850. A sympathetic porch has replaced the parked Mini outside no. 18 and the chimney-stack has been lowered.

Neithrop Hospital, the former Banbury Workhouse, February 1975. The workhouse, designed by Sampson Kempthorne and built by the Banbury firm Danby and Taylor, was in use by the end of 1835. A tramps' ward formerly existed behind the wall in the foreground and Arthur Jones recalled local characters such as Badger, Shuffler and Shiny Halfpenny queueing outside for overnight accommodation. After the end of the Poor Law system in 1929 the buildings were used as a hospital.

A 'turn left' sign in Warwick Road and a section of walling opposite are the only elements of continuity in a transformed scene. The Neithrop Hospital site was vacated in 1991 when all hospital facilities in Banbury were transferred to the Horton. The site has since been cleared and is now occupied by the Parklands housing estate.

Road improvements at the junction of Wood Green Avenue and Mascord Road, 1967. Wood Green Avenue was built in the mid-1950s as part of an inner ring road from Bloxham Road to Southam Road; from the beginning it was a dual carriageway with a wide grassy central reservation. It takes its name from the nearby Victorian house in Broughton Road built for Charles Gillett, the Banbury banker. Mascord Road was added in the early 1960s.

The growth of trees and shrubs has softened the appearance of Mascord Road, even in winter. At the same time increasing traffic has led to a proliferation of road signs and road markings and the introduction of a 20 m.p.h. speed limit in Mascord Road.

Quagmire above Stanbridge Close, 1966. Spaciously laid out, the houses on the north and east side of Bretch Hill backed on to the slope of the hill, which was retained in its semi-natural state with mature trees. The muddy back road continued the rural theme but the concrete lighting columns introduced a jarringly urban note.

The road is now fully made up and fenced to deter motorists from driving on to the adjacent grassland. Some of the old trees have been felled but recent planting is already making a visual impact on Bretch Hill.

The Mayor of Banbury hands over the keys of 116 Edmunds Road to a family from London, 1964. Part of Neithrop was soon called 'Little London' because so many newcomers had moved in; another area was known as 'The Aviary' because Bird's workers from Birmingham settled there.

Sylvia Gillard, a resident of Edmunds Road for thirty years, stands in the same doorway today.

Mothers and children enjoy the playground next to Woodfield on the Evenlode estate, 1973. In the early 1960s Banbury Borough Council signed 'overspill' agreements with London and Birmingham, launching a major expansion of the town as part of its plan to diversify the local economy. New estates off the Warwick Road housed many of the incoming families.

The 1970s playground, a scene of fun and probably a few tears, has been moved and segregated from dogs; the play equipment is perhaps tamer and the surface less likely to remove the skin from a child's knees. Hedges, shrubs and young trees give the area a more mature appearance.

CHAPTER SEVEN

CANAL & RAILWAY

Tooley's Boatyard on the Oxford Canal, 1970s. The boatyard was opened in 1790, just twelve years after the canal opened to Banbury, and narrow boats were built there until commercial traffic declined in the 1930s; since then, the yard has specialised in repair and refurbishment. At the point where the canal narrows a wooden drawbridge carried Factory Street across the water until the late 1960s.

Operated until 1998 by Morse Marine, Tooley's Boatyard is now empty, pending refurbishment as part of the development of a new Banbury Museum. The new Castle Quay Shopping Centre is rapidly taking shape beyond the boatyard and the bus station.

Narrow boats moored above Banbury Lock, 1970s. Castle Street bus station was built in 1968, clearing away Banbury Wharf and exposing Mill Lane to view in the background. Station Mill is visible away to the left.

The Castle Quay Shopping Centre development beginning in 1998 has further transformed the scene. Mill Lane, first recorded in 1407, has vanished and large-scale demolition in Bridge Street provides temporary views of buildings on the south side of the street. The bus station will be moved as the development proceeds.

The derelict Alpe's Factory seen across the canal in 1971. The tall building with the arched window was built in 1838 as a girth factory for Cobb's, a firm that could trace its origins back to 1701. Banbury Tweed Company occupied the premises from 1871 to 1902 and the Wyvern Kid Company made specialist leather there for a time. The buildings were used for the manufacture of aeroplane parts during the First World War, but had been empty for some years when Alpe Brothers acquired them in 1928 for the manufacture of furniture.

Chamberlaine Court now occupies this historic industrial site, bringing an attractive neo-Victorian look to the canal above Banbury Lock. A new Banbury Museum is to be built on the canalside beyond Chamberlaine Court.

Banbury Mill, 1970. The buildings date from the eighteenth century but the mill is perhaps on the same site as the Bishop of Lincoln's mill recorded 500 years earlier. Between 1878 and 1961 the mill was operated by the firm Edmunds & Kench, and on his way to and from the 'Rec' Arthur Jones saw sacks of corn being hoisted up into the building and horses being watered in the nearby stream. He also recalled the flock of Rhode Island Red hens that climbed a plank to their roost in the stores every evening.

One of Banbury Borough Council's last decisions was to establish a Spiceball Park Leisure Centre based in and around the old Banbury Mill. The Mill Arts Centre opened in 1974 and other facilities were added in 1977. Recreational use of the nearby mill meadow goes back to 1867 when a private company established a park and swimming bath, which the Borough Council took over in 1889. The unusual name Spiceball is said to derive from the spicy faggots made by a Bridge Street butcher, Mr Waddoups.

The Struggler pub on the corner of Mill Lane and Mill Street, 1965. Kept for many years by Mrs Soden, the Struggler was a very basic pub with sawdust on the floor; the original pub sign showed Atlas struggling to hold up the world on his shoulders. Marjory Lester remembered it as the canal boatmen's favourite pub and the sound of accordion music would often be heard in the evenings.

The steel frame of the Castle Quay Shopping Centre in November 1998, burying forever a secretive corner of old Banbury. When fitting out his narrow boat 'Cressy' for a canal expedition in the late 1930s, L.T.C. Rolt found it difficult to retrace his steps to Tooley's Boatyard and he spoke to local people who seemed unaware of the canal's existence.

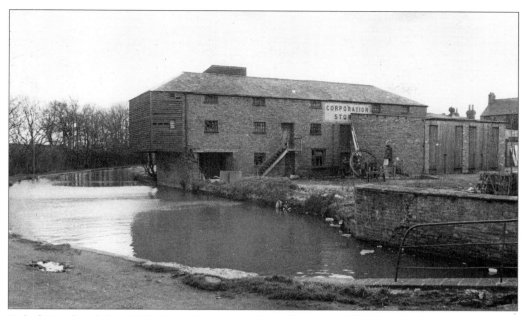

Oxford Canal and the old Banbury Corporation Store, January 1975. This wharf, approached from Mill Lane, was established in 1825 by the newly formed Banbury Paving and Lighting Commissioners to receive stone and other materials. Banbury Corporation inherited the wharf in 1889 and continued to use it until local government reorganisation in 1974.

Bluebird Bridge carrying Concord Avenue across the Oxford Canal. The building of Banbury's inner relief road obliterated the Corporation Wharf in 1990–1 and Concord Avenue now provides a northward continuation of Cherwell Street, carrying traffic to and from Hennef Way. The bridge is named after the former Blue Bird Commercial Temperance Hotel which flourished in Bridge Street between the wars.

Clark's Mill, or Station Mill, from the canal bridge in Bridge Street, 1962. Thomas Clark had the mill built in 1911 in a position that was convenient for transport by canal, railway or road. It was also powered by electricity from the power station in nearby Lower Cherwell Street. The mill supplied high grade flour to the country's leading biscuit manufacturers such as Huntley & Palmer's, Crawford's and Cadbury's. It was a noisy neighbour for local residents and covered the area with a fine dusting of white flour.

The ruins of Clark's Mill, which was largely destroyed in a spectacular fire on 16 March 1992. Clark's flour mill was the last of Banbury's mills to remain in production and its closure in March 1962 represented the end of an era. The impressive building was renovated and converted for the Altovar printing works in 1991 but it was gutted by fire within six months.

Merton Street station when it was part of the London, Midland and Scottish Railway Company network. The Buckinghamshire Railway, later subsumed into the London and North Western Railway, opened its line to Banbury on 1 May 1850, beating the GWR by a few months. The line remained a comparatively peaceful backwater, and in the early 1900s local children enjoyed waving at 'Slow Mary Janes', the locomotives of the South Midland Junction Railway.

Merton Street station survived nationalisation, and from 13 August 1956 British Railways experimented with diesel multiple units to encourage use of the line to Brackley and Buckingham. The service continued to lose money, however, and the last train passenger train left Merton Street on 31 December 1960. A warehouse now occupies the site of the station.

The Great Western Railway station from Station Road, *c*. 1900. Great Western services reached Banbury on 2 September 1850 with the opening of the line to Oxford; the extension to Birmingham was opened on 1 October 1852. The station was an unlikely venue for promenade concerts in 1851 and 1852 and a buffet was once served on the platform for Queen Victoria when her train stopped briefly on the way to Balmoral.

The present railway station, built by British Railways between 1956 and 1958. The GWR station was very shabby in later years and the overall roof above the platforms admitted snow and rain through the smoke vents on to waiting passengers. Its successor, delayed first by war and then by postwar austerity, cost about £500,000 and displayed a striking confidence in the future of the railways which Dr Beeching was soon to dispel.

Officials and photographers gather to mark the departure of the first Great Western rail-motor from Banbury to Bicester, July 1910. These trains could be driven from either end, the driver having a compartment at the front of the coach for the return journey. Arthur Jones and his school friends called the equivalent Kingham service the 'Chippy Chocolate' because of its brown and cream livery.

A Thames Trains Sprinter, the modern equivalent of the rail-motor, waits at platform 4, with the stopping service to Oxford and Reading.

The 'hump' marshalling yard, *c.* 1970. Built by the Great Western Railway in 1931 as an 'extensive gravitation yard for expediting the transfer of freight traffic', this facility made Banbury an important rail freight centre. Six days and nights a week, with Sunday as a day of rest for employees and nearby residents alike, wagons from the Midlands and the north-east were sorted into new train formations before being hauled to their destinations.

British Rail closed the 'hump' yard in May 1970 as a response to the steady decline in rail freight. The site is now occupied by the Middleton Meadows housing development.

CHAPTER EIGHT

GRIMSBURY & NETHERCOTE

The Elephant and Castle pub in Middleton Road, *c.* 1910. This seventeenth-century ironstone building has been a pub since about 1850; it was formerly Spital Farm and it stands on the site of medieval hospital of St Leonard. When the Great Western Railway Company extended its line through Banbury it transferred the licence from the nearby disreputable Golden Lion pub to this old farmhouse and built a new farmhouse further south.

The Elephant and Castle has a 1920s extension but the old building has changed little; a redundant chimney-stack has been removed from the gable end and a second dormer window of sympathetic design has been added. The railings around the nearby public toilets were probably taken away for scrap during the Second World War.

Merton Street, 1970s. Begun in the 1870s, Merton Street was a quiet residential street on the southern edge of Grimsbury until Midland Marts Ltd opened their cattle market near the LMS railway station in 1925. Subsequently local residents had to cope with herds of cattle and later with cattle trucks on market days.

The expansion of Banbury Cattle Market to become the largest cattle market in Europe by the 1970s led to the demolition of houses on the south side of Merton Street. With the opening of the M40 in 1991, the future prosperity of Banbury Cattle Market seemed assured but it closed down suddenly in June 1998, bringing to an end the age-old link between the town and its rural hinterland.

Demolition contractors move in to clear Grimsbury Council School, *c.* 1996. The attractive brick building, with separate entrances for boys, girls and infants, was erected in 1910 to accommodate 600 children in the growing area. James Dommett was the school's first headmaster and the infants' mistress was Eliza Wells.

The school had a varied history, becoming a secondary modern school and then a subsidiary of Banbury School before ending its days as St Leonard's Junior School. It closed with some regrets on 10 February 1995 and the site was sold for housing to help pay for the new Grimsbury St Leonard's School in Overthorpe Road. Traditional brick houses in Old School Place and School View now occupy the site.

A delivery of Hooky ale to the Bowling Green pub at Nethercote, June 1987. This little roadside pub dates perhaps from the eighteenth century and its bowling green became a cricket ground in Victorian times; a quiet country walk beyond Grimsbury, it was the destination for many works outings from Banbury. The nearby First World War munitions factory drastically changed the pub's outlook for a time but this was abandoned in the 1920s and the Bowling Green remained detached from the expanding town.

The Bowling Green pub lost its rural aspect in 1988–91 when the M40 was built alongside. A bridge carries Overthorpe Road over the motorway but few of today's Banbury residents perhaps will make the pub the destination for a country stroll.

Middleton Road, 1920s. The block of houses behind the parked car included the Grimsbury Corn Stores, Annie Southam's drug store and Strouds' butcher's shop. Strouds' slaughtered animals in the yard behind their shop and delivered meat all over town in a smart green pony trap. Further on, the Cricketers pub at no. 41 was a reminder of a former cricket ground at the back which was the County School's sports ground in the 1920s.

Alldays now occupy 35/39 Middleton Road and traffic lights control the junction with the access road to the Middleton Meadow development on the site of the Banbury 'hump' marshalling yard. The name Waterloo Drive harks back to the early nineteenth-century Waterloo Cottages that stood near Banbury Bridge; described as the home of rogues by the local historian William Potts, they were cleared away by the Great Western Railway as it extended its line through Banbury.

Duke Street, 1970s. Built by William Wilkins in the 1860s with bricks from his own adjacent brickyard, the street was a row of thirty identical two-up, two-down houses; Marjory Lester remembered a tin bath hanging outside each back door and a toilet at the end of each garden. The former brickworks became an area of wasteland at the end of the street, serving as the neighbourhood tip and as a great place for local children to explore.

The old Duke Street was cleared in the 1980s and the site is now occupied by two blocks of flats, Guardian Court and Northumberland Court, and by the necessary parking spaces.

Grimsbury Methodist Church, West Street, celebrates its centenary in 1971. The Wesleyans opened a small chapel in North Street in 1858 and the growth of the congregation in Grimsbury led to the building of the West Street chapel in 1871. In the 1930s the church was packed out on Sundays with a large Sunday School in the mornings and an Adult School in the afternoons. Meetings, social clubs and Methodist Band rehearsals were held there on weekdays.

The old building became unsuitable for contemporary needs and a modern Grimsbury Methodist Church, built in 1986, now stands in West Street.

West Street, looking north towards the distant Our House beerhouse and off-licence on the corner of North Street, 1920s. Just one pedestrian brings life to a street with considerable architectural variety. The Banbury Freehold Land Society purchased the site of New Grimsbury, originally Freetown, in 1851 and provided 151 plots for small-scale speculative building. These two- and three-storey brick houses were erected in the 1850s and 1860s.

A few houses have rendered or stone-cladded façades but the fabric of West Street has changed little. Now that most households have access to a car, the street is lined with vehicles and the narrowing of the carriageway on the right is part of a traffic-calming scheme.

The Prince of Wales pub on the corner of Centre Street and South Street, *c.* 1930. The Prince of Wales, located at the heart of the Freehold Land Society estate, was described as newly built in 1855; between the wars it was owned by the brewers Hopcrafts of Brackley.

Rendered and painted walls made the pub stand out from its brick neighbours but the foodless 'local' has lost its appeal and the building is currently being converted into flats. The trees and shrubs in the foreground are a traffic-calming device, making Centre Street into a peaceful cul-de-sac.

Ladders Lane in Old Grimsbury, *c.* 1910. The lane passing these picturesque country cottages continued to Grimsbury Manor and across the railway to Field's Mill and Banbury Waterworks.

The curve of Manor Road and the distant trees are surviving elements in a much-changed scene. The old stone cottages, remembered as being very poky inside, have given way to modern suburban houses.

Grimsbury Manor, 1970s. This attractive house replaced the old manor house that was demolished in 1836. Remembered for its beautiful wooded gardens and for its springtime display of snowdrops, daffodils and lilac blossom, the manor house was formerly the home of Lamley Fisher, a local solicitor. In the 1950s a man nicknamed 'Holy Joe' lived there and grew vegetables for sale.

The building of Hennef Way in 1990–1 claimed the fountain in front of the manor house and most of the garden as well. After a period of neglect Grimsbury Manor faces a new future as part of an office complex.

Waterworks Lane, 1977. An obsolete Borough of Banbury notice and a 15 m.p.h. speed limit sign guard the approach to the waterworks from Old Grimsbury. The Banbury Water Company established its waterworks here in 1857, taking water from the river Cherwell near Grimsbury Mill.

Waterworks Lane has been widened and, with traffic hurrying along nearby Hennef Way, it no longer seems remote. The lane itself remains quiet, however, and it is a gateway to the Spiceball Country Park that extends south into the heart of Banbury between the Cherwell and the Oxford Canal.